Run Your R

D0254357

A Look at the Business Strategies of 20 Top Rappers

By Curtis Marshall

Minute Help Press

www.minutehelp.com

Table of Contents

While most think of Rap as an entertainment medium, the reality that it is also as much of a business as any Fortune 500 company. Rappers seek to market their brand by creating quality songs, or products. The richest rappers take this a step further and use the brand they have built in music as an advantage in their business ventures, and that is where this book comes in.

This book will describe the surprising business acumen of the rappers profiled, and will provide you with detailed descriptions of how they became wealthy beyond their hit singles. Some business ventures that will be discussed include: 50 Cent and Vitamin Water, Sean John and Rocawear by Diddy and Jay Z, a diamond mine owned by Akon, and a brand of wines by Lil Jon. As you will see, many rappers are excellent businessmen and much can be learned from their strategies for success.

Shawn "Jay-Z" Carter

Net Worth: 450 million

While Jay Z is one of the most successful rap artists of all time, he has also made quite a splash in the business world. Mr. Carter's first business venture was Roc-a-fella Records, which he created in the 90's when no major record label would sign him. In 1997 he sold half of Roc-a-Fella for 1.5 million, and he sold the other half in 2004 for 10 million. Jay Z's first non-music related venture was Roca wear clothing line, which he founded in 1999.

In a truly savvy business move, he sold Roca wear to Iconix for 204 million, but still managed to maintain control of the marketing, creative direction, and product development for the men's Roca wear line. His other business ventures include: a minority share in the New Jersey Nets, owner of the 40/40 upscale sports club, and co-brand director of Budweiser select.

Shawn " Jay Z" Carter is one of the most successful businessmen in the rap industry, and there are a couple of reasons why this is the case. The first is that Jay Z understands the concept of branding better than any rapper in the industry. Early on in his career, he asked himself " What do I want people to think of when they hear Jay Z?" He essentially answered this when his 1996 album, Reasonable Doubt, was a huge hit with the urban hip-hop demographic but not with the much bigger and more lucrative pop audience. Jay Z's next album produced a bunch of pop hits and brought the Jay Z brand to a much wider market. The lesson here is that you must create your brand with the goal of targeting as wide of a market as possible. Jay Z realized that being known specifically as a hardcore gangster rapper would limit his reach and instead altered his brand image to reach a wider audience.

Jay Z is also very talented at remaining actively involved in all of his business ventures, rather than simply playing the role of investor. He summed up this philosophy best in his verse on the remix to Kanye West's Diamonds of Sierra Leone, which says, "I'm not a businessman; I'm a business, man." A big part of what makes Jay Z a great businessman is his desire to be fully involved in all the important aspects of his business. This is a great quality for a CEO to have since a personable CEO can serve as a trustworthy face for a brand and develop the all-important customer loyalty.

Jay Z also utilizes brand affiliation any chance he gets. A good example of this is his partnership with Budweiser Select, in which he was named co-creative director in 2006. He appeared in a commercial that had "Show Me What You Got" playing, which was the single of his soon to be released album at the time. This affiliation promoted Budweiser's product to Jay Z fans, and in turn Jay Z was exposed to Budweiser's market, which contains demographics that Jay Z would not reach otherwise.

Finally, Jay Z is great at knowing what his market wants. He has a line in a song that goes "I dumbed down my lyrics just to double my dollars," referring to the shift in image he made between his first and second album. This is great business advice because it is essentially saying that you have to provide a product or service that is truly wanted or needed by your target market.

With that being said, here are ten strategies that Jay Z uses that you can apply to your own business ventures:

- Know what you want people to think of when they think of your brand
- Be in tune with your target audience
- Be hands-on in all of your business ventures
- Affiliate with other brands to expose your brand to new markets
- Be open to new and unorthodox ideas
- Always look for new mediums to expand your brand
- Develop and trust your business intuition
- Fully commit to any decision you make

- Surround yourself with successful businessmen to serve as a trustworthy source for advice
- Make sure your main priority is providing a product or service that your target customer truly wants

Sean "Diddy" Combs

Net Worth: 475 million

Sean Combs, better known by his stage name Diddy, is one of the original hip-hop entrepreneurs, and also one of the wealthiest. In 2010, he made 30 million dollars through numerous business ventures. Diddy is the owner of the record label Bad Boy Records, where he gave fame to the late Notorious B.I.G. Outside of music, Diddy owns an upscale restaurant in Atlanta called Justin's. He is also creative director, lead of marketing, and 50-50 partner in Ciroc vodka. In addition to music and business, Diddy has an acting career. He has starred on Broadway in A Raisin in the Sun, and starred as himself in Get Him to the Greek.

There is a reason why Sean "Diddy" Combs wants to open a business school in Harlem, and it is because he is one of the best businessmen in the hip-hop industry. One strategy that he has been using since the beginning of his career is brand affiliation. Although Diddy has come out with a couple of his own albums that have sold well, he knew that he did not have the lyrical talents of other up and coming rappers of the 90's. He knew that to maximize his success he needed to affiliate with a more talented rapper, who turned out to be Notorious B.I.G., signing Biggie to be his "launch product" for Bad Boy Records. By collaborating with Biggie on a few songs, which is musical brand affiliation, Diddy was able to further the success of his own brand.

More recently, Diddy used brand affiliation to become partners with Diageo, the company that owns Ciroc vodka. Since Diddy became a partner the Vodka has seen a 552% profit increase in the U.S. market. By doing this, Diddy exposes himself to a new market and increases his brand's reach. Diddy was able to secure a 50-50 partnership by knowing exactly how much he is worth to the company.

Another trait that makes Diddy a successful businessman is that he is great at being the face of his brand. Diddy's venture with Ciroc vodka is a great example of this. This can be a great strategy for any business, especially small businesses. By being the face of your brand, potential customers are more likely to buy your product, since it feels like they are buying from a person and not a faceless conglomerate.

Diddy is also an expert at integrating his products into the lifestyle of his targeted demographic. Essentially what this means is that Diddy uses himself as a free advertisement by always using products that he sells. For example, Diddy tweets constantly about Ciroc vodka and its different flavors, as well as different drink recipes. The message Diddy is trying to get across to his audience is that people can be more like him if they buy his products.

Diddy is able to do all of these things because he has the ability to remain extremely focused on completing any goal he set for himself. Even though Diddy grew up in poverty, when asked if he ever knew he would become rich he always replies "yes." It is this dedication to vision that has served as the formula of Diddy's business success.

If you like Diddy's business strategies, then check out these top 10 ways to run your business like Diddy.

- Always look for ways to affiliate your brand to maximize success
- Remain dedicated to a goal until it is accomplished
- Believe that you cannot fail
- Use people who don't agree with your idea to motivate yourself toward success
- Be the face of your brand
- Know what your target market is looking for
- Associate your brand with a specific lifestyle
- Cross-Promote products with an affiliate
- Always enjoy running your business
- Remain updated on the newest market trends

Aliuane "Akon" Thiam

Net Worth: 45 million

According to Forbes, Akon made 21 million dollars in 2010, which was from music as well as other business ventures. Within the music industry Akon owns two record labels, Konvict Muzik and Kon live, which are home to T Pain and Lady Gaga respectively.

Outside of the music industry, Akon owns two clothing lines. His Konvict clothing line is targeted to the urban demographic, while his Aliuane clothing line is targeted towards the high end fashion market. Akon also owns a diamond mine in Sierra Leone, which is a truly unique business venture in the rap industry.

Aliuane " Akon" Thiam is an up and coming name in the hip-hop industry and has already had great success due to his ability to market the Akon brand. When Akon first broke into the hip hop industry, he maximized his exposure by using brand affiliation. He is credited with over 300 guest appearances on other songs, which is a great example of Akon affiliating with more established brands. This is a great strategy because the affiliation with established artists gives him instant credibility. Another benefit is that he exposes his brand to many different markets.

Another strategy that Akon uses is exploiting an untapped niche. Akon is a singer rather than a rapper, so he is perfect for singing the chorus, or " hook", of a rap song. Essentially, Akon built his brand by establishing and exploiting a niche market, which in his case is being a singer in the rap industry. Developing a product or service for a niche market can be a very profitable marketing strategy if used correctly.

Akon also knows how to spot talent, as he is the one who gave both T Pain and Lady Gaga their first record deals. In terms of business strategy, what Akon does is judge what product (or in this case artist) will sell best to the target audience. For success in business it is vital to be able to accurately judge what will sell in your market.

Akon also has a great strategy when it comes to investments. When asked about why he invested in a diamond mine, his reply was that people will always be getting married so diamonds will always be in demand. This is an excellent strategy to follow for any type of investment. Before committing any capital, evaluate whether the product or service you are investing in is a fad or something with a long shelf life.

Finally, Akon knows how to build a brand image with the best of them. While it is true that Akon has had some trouble with the law, he has drastically overplayed this fact to give his brand the urban edge that the market demands. His first single was even titled " Locked Up," which is about his life in jail.

Overall, Akon is a great musician and a marketing genius, so here are 10 tips from Akon that you can use in your business ventures.

- Brand collaboration is a great way to gain exposure
- Exploit a niche market
- Think long term when making investments
- Be a great reader of your target market
- Diversify your business within your industry (i.e. Akon has two record labels and two clothing lines for different demographics within the same industry)
- Always be conscious of your brand image in relation to your target market
- If you feel a unique product or service has potential, give it a chance
- Stay committed to your product
- Constantly seek more exposure
- Make sure your image caters to customer expectations

Dwayne "Lil Wayne" Carter

Net Worth: 85 Million

With a net worth of 85 million and having already made 15 million in 2011, Lil Wayne is quickly establishing himself as one of the richest rappers in the music industry. Lil Wayne signed to Cash Money Records when he was just nine years old, and has since founded his own label, Young Money Records, which has produced stars like Drake and Nikki Minaj. Lil Wayne plans to launch a champagne called Halo as well as a clothing line, which will be called Rebirth.

Lil Wayne is on his way to becoming one of the richest rappers in the industry without launching any business ventures, but he has plans to enter the business world with Halo champagne and Rebirth clothing. Lil Wayne has already proved his good business sense by postponing his original 2008 release of his champagne indefinitely. Lil Wayne realized that, because of the recession, the market was bad for everything, especially a luxury item like champagne. The marketing strategy that Lil Wayne is using here is waiting for the right time to enter the market. As anyone who has tried to market a product or service knows, timing is everything. Your product could have an amazing and engaging marketing campaign, but even the best campaign can't sell a luxury item in a recession.

Another reason why Lil Wayne is so successful is that he re-invented the strategy behind mix tapes. Mix tapes are simply a collection of songs that an artist releases for free. Lil Wayne realized that by releasing mix tapes a couple months before an album, he could build hype for his album and increase his sales. The same type of concept can be applied to any business in the form of free trials. By offering to let customers try your product or service for free before a purchase, you can gain the customer's trust.

Lil Wayne is also an expert at using social media to market his content. He showed the power of his social media reach when Oreo set a world record for the amount of likes on a single Facebook post with 114,619 likes, and Lil Wayne broke it with a post that got 588,243 likes. This example shows how far his social media reach extends, as well as the brand loyalty he has built with his fans.

Here are 10 strategies from Lil Wayne that you can use while running your business.

- Be unique
- Provide customers with a free trial
- Evaluate the economy before releasing a product
- Master social media to maximize your reach
- Know what your market wants
- Build customer loyalty through good content marketing
- Strive to provide the best product in your industry
- Be the face of your brand
- Collaborate with other brands to maximize exposure

- Remember that in marketing, timing is everything

Andre "Dr. Dre" Young

Net Worth: 125 Million

With a net worth of 125 million and 17 million in earnings in 2010, all without releasing an album in a decade, it is clear that Dr. Dre is a great businessman. Dr. Dre is much better known as a producer than a rapper, and helped propel Snoop Dogg, 50 Cent, and Eminem to stardom. In addition to his record label, Aftermath Entertainment, Dr. Dre also has headphones called Beats by Dre. He also plans on releasing a cognac called Aftermath when he releases his new album " Detox" sometime in 2011.

The fact that Dr. Dre has accumulated a net worth of 125 million without releasing an album in 10 years shows his talents as a businessman. He has had success as a rapper, but he realized he was much better at making beats, which is why he chose to stick to the producing side of rap.

Although he has not dropped an album in 10 years, during that time he made stars out of Snoop Dogg, Eminem, and 50 cent. In a sense, Dr. Dre is similar to a bigger parent company that buys smaller companies and then increases their popularity by using their resources to develop the smaller brand. Dr. Dre. Has produced three " Brands" that are on the Forbes list of 20 richest rappers. If you are a big business that can afford to buy smaller businesses with potential, then you should buy them and develop them using the success blueprint of the parent company.

Dr. Dre has also shown good business technique outside of the music industry with his line of headphones, called Beats by Dre. First off, he branched into a new business that was still music related. This is a great strategy since his career as a rapper and producer gives him credibility when trying to sell headphones. A good way to expand your wealth is to explore a new market that allows you to use your previous business ventures as an advantage.

Dr. Dre also uses brand affiliation by having Lady Gaga come out with headphones, called Heartbreakers by Dre. By doing this Dre profits from a demographic that he would have never reached if it weren't for brand affiliation. Try to affiliate with a business that isn't competing with you in the same demographic.

Dr. Dre is an expert at finding businesses to collaborate with. For example, he has collaborated with HP to sell a Beats by Dre laptop that also includes a pair of his headphones. Dr. Dre knows that a partnership with a computer company is good business because most people use their computer to listen to music. Another example is Dr. Dre's partnership with Chrysler, which will have the 2012 Chrysler 300 equipped with a Beats by Dre sound system.

Dr. Dre is a business genius and here are 10 strategies he has used for success.

- Invest in smaller companies with high potential
- Expose yourself to as many markets as possible

- Get involved in business ventures where your experience can be an advantage
- Collaborate with business's that aren't part of the competition
- Don't release a new product until the current product has lost all value
- Try to target both genders
- Partner with other businesses in industries that relate to yours
- Know that there are many ways to make money, but only one way to make the most money
- Personally endorse your product
- Back up your advertising claims with quality product

Christopher "Ludacris" Bridges

Net Worth: 60 Million

In addition to a successful career as a hip-hop artist, Ludacris is the CEO of Disturbing the Peace Records, which has signed other Southern rappers such as Chingy and Shawwna. Outside of the music industry Ludacris owns Straits restaurant in midtown Atlanta and has a 50-50 partnership in a cognac called Conjure. Ludacris also has a clothing line called CP Time and a brand of high-end headphones called Soul. Outside of the business world, Ludacris has had a successful acting career, appearing in movies such as Hustle & Flow, Gamer, and the Fast and the Furious series.

As Ludacris' career has progressed, one thing that has made him successful is being conscious of his image. When Ludacris first burst on to the scene, his lyrics were filled with degrading lines toward women, which is common in some forms of rap. When Ludacris realized that this was giving him a negative image in some circles, he thought of the concept for his most recent album entitled Battle of the Sexes. Almost every song on this album features a duet with a female hip hop artist. Ludacris did this to repair his image in the female demographic and prove he was more than a rapper who degraded women.

An important business lesson can be learned from this, and that is to counter any negative opinion about your brand with something positive. Listen to your customer's complaints and try to fix them as fast as possible.

Ludacris has also succeeded in evolving his brand as his market evolved. Sometime in the early 2000's, rap fans shifted from wanting to hear gangster rapper to wanting rap with a better message. As the market shifted so did Ludacris, which is evident if you compare his first album with his most recent.

Ludacris also showed good business sense when he partnered with Jimmy Yeo, an executive chef and owner of a chain of restaurants in the bay area, to open his own Singaporean restaurant called Straits. Ludacris sought someone who has already had success in the industry he planned on entering, and that is part of the reason why he has been successful. This strategy can work for anyone in the business world as long as you remember that there is no shame in asking for help.

Finally, Ludacris knows the importance of portraying a product as a status enhancer. With his cognac, Conjure, Ludacris wanted to provide an affordable version of a liquor usually reserved for the upper class. By doing this, Ludacris' strategy is to target the middle to lower class with an item that will make them feel like they are a part of the upper class.

Here are 10 tips to help you run your business like Ludacris.

- Always be aware of your image
- Counter negative press with positive press
- Don't be afraid to ask for advice

- Seek a mentor if you're venturing into unfamiliar territory
- Your brand should evolve with the market
- Market your product as a status enhancer
- Use social media to build a connection with your customers
- Never get complacent
- Don't become too predictable
- Seek partnerships that will be beneficial to your business ventures

Calvin "Snoop Dogg" Broadus

Net Worth: 130 Million

Snoop Dogg has been in the rap industry for almost 20 years and shows no sign of slowing down, managing to make 15 million in 2010. He has just recently started his own label, which is called Dogg Town Music Group. Snoop Dogg also has his hands in other ventures, like headphones with Skullcandy, and Blast malt liquor with Colt 45. He also serves as a spokesman for Chrysler and Sundrop soda. In addition to business ventures, Snoop has appeared in movies like Starsky & Hutch and Training Day.

Most rappers aren't able to produce a successful second album, let alone still be dropping albums 20 years after their debut. Snoop Dogg has realized that he is a brand and that any decision he makes can positively or negatively affect his brand. When Snoop Dogg first blew up in 1993, he was the perfect fit for the gangster rap persona since he served a few years in prison. At that time the gangster rapper was a popular brand so his image worked; however, when the gangster rap image faded Snoop Dogg quickly cleaned up his image. A valuable business lesson to be taken from this is that it is important to know what type of image customers expect from your brand.

Another reason why Snoop Dogg is so successful is that he is unique. He dresses uniquely, and even speaks uniquely compared to other rappers. Being unique is an important marketing strategy as the average customer tends to embrace individuality in a brand rather than adhering to the status quo. Always strive to display your brand as offering something that only your brand can offer.

Snoop Dogg is also excellent at remaining focused. He is dedicated to expanding his reach and maximizing his profit, which shows in his numerous business ventures. For example, in 2003 Snoop released " Snoop Doggs," which were Snoop Dogg branded hot dogs. While the venture was short lived, it exemplifies Snoop Dogg's dedication to expanding in untapped markets.

Snoop Dogg is one of the rap industry's greatest businessmen, and here are 10 strategies he used to get where he is today.

- Be unique
- Know what image your customer expects from your brand
- Your brand should evolve with the market
- Never lose your passion
- Don't second guess your idea, no matter how far fetched
- Build good partnerships with other successful brands
- Remain completely involved in anything attached to your brand

- Always look for untapped markets to exploit
- Always remain focused on your goal
- Learn from your failures to ensure they will not happen again

Timothy "Timbaland" Mosley

Net Worth: 75 Million

While Timbaland has yet to follow the path of other rappers and branch off into the business world, he has accumulated great wealth from the music industry. Timbaland got his start in the early 90's when he produced R&B stars Aliyiah and Genuwine's debut albums. Timbaland also released his first rap album around that time with his partner Magoo. Timbaland continued his success by producing songs for seemingly everybody in the music industry, having collaborated with names like Missy Elliot, Justin Timberlake, Nelly Furtado, Madonna, Britney Spears, and Miley Cyrus.

Even though Timbaland doesn't have as many business ventures, he is still one of the best businessmen in the rap industry. The fact that he has established a net worth of 75 million shows that he has succeeded greatly in marketing the Timbaland brand. A strategy Timbaland committed to early on in his career is completely dominating a niche, which in his case is producing. While Timbaland still raps, he has committed himself more to producing because he knows he is an excellent producer compared to an average rapper.

What Timbaland did here was identify his strengths and how they can best be used to develop his brand. This strategy should be part of the business plan of any business just getting started, since knowing the strengths of yourself and your product will maximize your chance of success. Timbaland established himself as one of the industry's best producers by diverging from the status quo of hip hop and R&B beats and developing his own unique sounds.

For example, Rap beats at the time were bass heavy with samples used from other songs. Timbaland preferred more electronic sounds and never used samples. This was a great strategy because any artist looking for a unique sound wants Timbaland to be their producer. It is a vital strategy for success to make sure your product is unique in the eye of the customer.

Timbaland is also a master of collaboration, or joint ventures, as they are known in the business world. By nature, a producer must be great at working with other brands (artists). Timbaland has also produced for artists outside of the hip hop industry, like Britney Spears and Miley Cyrus. His album Shockwave 2 featured artists such as Britney Spears, Justin Timberlake, and Nelly Furtado. As a business owner, it is important to always be on the lookout for joint ventures that will help your business.

Here are 10 strategies for success from Timbaland that you can use in your business.

- Be creative
- Always market your product with a unique angle

- Trust your intuition when doing something unorthodox
- Find a niche in your market and dominate it
- Associate yourself with successful brands
- Make sure you get the most out of your business relationship
- Try to revolutionize your industry
- Be a leader not a follower
- Know what your audience wants
- Identify the strengths of both you and your product and use it to your advantage

Pharrell Williams

Net Worth: 77.5 Million

Pharrell Williams is part of the alternative rock group N.E.R.D as well as half of the producing duo the Neptunes. While Pharrell has achieved great success in all of his music ventures, he has also been successful in the business world. IN 2008, Pharrell designed a line of jewelry and sunglasses for Louis Vuitton. He also has his own clothing line named Billionaire Boys Club, as well as a sneaker line called the Ice Cream shoe collection. Recently, he has invested in a company called Bionic Yarn, who are dedicated to use green methods in producing textiles.

Pharrell is unique in the music industry because he has the ability to transcend demographics like nobody else in the rap industry. The Pharrell brand has reach in the rock demographic with his group N.E.R.D. and the hip hop market with the Neptunes. This strategy of appealing to multiple demographics is a great move for your brand if you can pull it off. Knowing your current and potential targeted demographics in and out is essential when using this strategy, as it is important to be able to predict whether or not your brand would fare well in a given demographic.

Pharrell recently made a move to become co-owner of Returns textile, which is a "green" textile made from recycled plastic bottles. This is a great strategy for the CEO that enjoys a little risk. The green industry also has the potential to become quite popular in the future. It is important to always evaluate the potential risks vs. the potential rewards of every investment.

Another strategy Pharrell uses for success is cross promoting his products. For example, Pharrell will promote his green textile company by using the textile for his Billionaire Boys Club clothing line. Another example is that he promotes his Ice Cream shoe collection by sponsoring the Ice Cream skate team.

Pharrell is also great at marketing products because he is dedicated to being the face of his product. For example, when Pharrell designed the jewelry and sunglass line for Louis Vuitton, he could have stopped there; however, he remained dedicated to being the spokesman to sell the line. If you can put a face behind your product you'll make customers feel like using your business is a personable experience. In turn, this will lead to improved customer trust and brand loyalty.

Here are 10 strategies Pharrell uses to be successful.

- Try and reach multiple demographics
- Be aware of current trends in the market
- Don't be afraid to invest in what you think could be the next big thing
- Trust your intuition
- Always look to cross promote your product
- Joint ventures are great for spreading brand awareness
- Be creative
- Don't shy away from a business venture just because people think it is unorthodox
- Be the face of your brand

- Look for ways to score brownie points with your customers

Kanye West

Net Worth: 70 Million

Kanye West began his career as a producer for Jay Z's record label, Roc-A-Fella Records. In 2004 he released his first solo album, and has since had all five of his albums go platinum. Kanye also has his own record label, G.O.O.D Music, which is home to artists such as Common, Kid Cudi, and John Legend. In addition to his music ventures, Kanye has his own fragrance and clothing line. Kanye also owns a chain of 10 Fatburger restaurants in his hometown of Chicago. He also has an energy drink called GURU that is all natural and organic.

Whether you love him or hate him, everybody has an opinion on Kanye West. Whatever your feelings on Kanye may be, anyone in marketing can see Kanye's arrogance and cockiness are all part of his marketing strategy. Kanye has complete and utter confidence in his business moves, which is a big advantage in the world of business. The one thing all successful CEOs have is complete faith that they will succeed. They never obsess over what can go wrong and instead focus all their energy into reaching their desired level of success.

Kanye West uses confidence to his advantage better than any other rapper. While his ego certainly turns some people away, it makes his fans absolutely love him. Kanye targets the people that embrace his style and pays little attention to criticism. This is a great strategy, as paying too close attention to criticism can cause you to second guess your ideas and become overly conservative. It is important to remember that no matter how great your product or service is, you can't please everybody.

Kanye West is also a genius at internet marketing. One of Kanye's internet marketing strategies is releasing a free song every Friday, which he has named G.O.O.D. Fridays. This alone dramatically increases traffic to his website, and he takes it a step further by requiring users to provide their email address to get access to the song. By doing this, Kanye has built an extensive mailing list that can be used to spread awareness of future business ventures. With 2.1 million followers, Kanye also uses Twitter for free and instant marketing. In today's digital age it is important to take advantage of email and social media to market your product since they are a free advertising medium.

Here are 10 strategies Kanye West uses to remain successful in the business world.

- Get your start under someone who has established themselves as a success
- There is no such thing as bad press
- Controversy can sell
- Have complete confidence in your ability to succeed
- Free products & promotions are a great way to build customer loyalty
- Trust your intuition

- Embrace individuality over conformity
- Pay very close attention to the wants of your target customer
- Don't pay too much attention to criticism
- Take advantage of the internet to market your brand

Aubrey "Drake" Graham

Net Worth: 10 million

Although Drake's net worth is lower than most others on the list, he is the industry's highest earning newcomer. Before he was a rapper Drake had already had a successful career as an actor starring on the show Degrassi as Jimmy. In 2006, Drake ventured into the music business by releasing a series of mix tapes that received praise from names like Jay Z, Kanye West, and Lil Wayne. In fact, Drake ended up signing with Lil Wayne on his Young Money record label. Although Drake has yet to get his feet wet in the business world, he has participated in advertising campaigns with Sprite and Virgin America.

Although it is not officially known, Drake's net worth is estimated to be around 10 million. Drake took the fast track to superstardom by generating massive amounts of buzz while being unsigned. He released mix tape after mix tape and had his song "Replacement Girl" featured on BET's Joint of the Day. When first entering the market, it is vital that you generate buzz about your business. One way to do this is to do what Drake did and release free content. A more business friendly version of this is the concept of the free trial and money back guarantee.

Drake also understood that he could spread his brand much faster by collaborating with people who have already had great success, like Jay Z and Lil Wayne. By getting such prominent names to endorse his brand, he set himself up to quickly increase his net worth. You should make a conscious effort to gain credible endorsements from experts in your industry when first starting. Potential customers will see this and be more likely to trust your brand.

Once Drake established worth in his brand, companies like Sprite and Virgin America wanted him to help sell their product. Essentially Drake went from having to seek out joint ventures to being sought after for joint ventures, which is a key indicator of success. When you start getting offers for joint ventures from other companies, you know you are on the right track.

Here are 10 strategies that Drake uses to be successful that you can also use in your own business ventures.

- Seek Endorsements from those established in the industry
- Provide free trials and money back guarantees
- Take advantage of every opportunity
- Be diverse in your strategies
- Collaborate with other brands to maximize your reach
- Trust your instincts
- Know your brand's worth
- Make your goal to be sought for joint ventures, and not having to seek them

- Market your brand to as many demographics as possible
- Keep your customers happy

Clifford "T.I." Harris

Net Worth: 35 Million

Musically, T.I. has recorded seven studio albums, all of which have been a success. He is also the CEO of his own record label, Grand Hustle Entertainment, which he formed in 2003 when he was dropped from his original label. He also has a successful acting career, starring in movies such as ATL, American Gangster, and Takers. Recently he has formed his own film production company called Grand Hustle films. In addition, T.I. owns Club Crucial in Atlanta, which is ranked among the city's hottest night clubs. T.I. is also creative consultant of Remy Martin Cognac and plans to release his own blend of the brand.

Perhaps the best lesson to be learned from T.I. is how to repair a damaged image. T.I. lost his endorsements from Axe and Remy Martin when he was sent to prison on federal gun charges, and then was sent back to prison for violating his parole with a drug possession. Realizing that his image was fast approaching irreparable, he tried to turn his image around by doing community service work revolving around lecturing kids on the dangers of drugs and guns. He has also helped with relief efforts for Hurricane Katrina, and has funded many scholarships for Boys and Girls clubs. The fact is that any business's image can suffer damage at any time, so it is important to have a strategy in place to repair the damage as quickly as possible.

T.I. also has good business sense as his nightclub, Club Crucial, is one of the most popular nightclubs in Atlanta. One reason for this success is that T.I. is an expert at running promotions. Most nights have a theme: Monday is open mic night, Fridays are free admission, and Celebrity Saturdays feature local hip hop artists performing. T.I. offers a great model for success, especially in running a bar or club. A great way to build a customer base is to offer a different special for each night of the week. If you want to widen your customer reach, try to appeal to a different demographic each day. For example, T.I. has open mic Monday to draw aspiring rappers to his club, free Fridays to draw those that are turned off by a cover charge, and Celebrity Saturdays for those looking to catch a glimpse of someone famous.

Even with his legal troubles, T.I. has remained one of the most successful men in the industry, so here are 10 strategies to run your business like T.I.

- Repair any damage to your image before it is too late
- Be active in your community
- Establish yourself as a philanthropic company

- Figure out ways around roadblocks
- Don't be afraid to be personable and show emotions in conversations with customers
- Always remain focused on success
- Master the concept of promotions, especially when running a bar or club
- Provide something for as many demographics as possible
- Use the internet to promote yourself and connect with customers
- Never stop trying to improve your image, especially if it has been damaged in the past

Kasseem "Swizz Beatz" Dean

Net Worth: 125 Million

Kasseem Dean, better known by his stage name Swizz Beatz, sold his first beat when he was 16 years old and has since become one of the rap industry's premiere producers. In 2001 he started his own record label, Full Surface, and gave rapper Cassidy a deal as his first signing. Swizz Beatz is also partners with Kidrobot, a company that sells art, toys, and apparel. In 2010, he partnered with Reebok to release his own sneaker line. Swizz Beatz also has sold paintings commercially.

One strategy that Kasseem " Swizz Beatz" Dean mastered very early on in his career is how to use connections. He had an uncle that worked for the Ruff Ryders label, which gave him his big break that gave him the chance to produce the eventual hit " Ruff Ryders Anthem" by DMX. This is a great strategy for any businessperson looking to rise in rank within their company. Form good relationships with those in high places, since you might need these endorsements when your big break comes around.

Swizz Beatz is also good at having established members of the industry to market himself. Ever since his first song with DMX, he has been producing for elite names in the hip hop industry. He has produced hits for names such as Beyoncé, T.I., Cassidy, Styles P, and Busta Rhymes. If you are trying to start a business, don't be afraid to seek a mentor to give you valuable advice and endorsements.

Swizz Beatz is also great at enhancing his image through philanthropic ventures. Any revenue he gains from selling his paintings he donates to the Child Cancer and Blood Foundation. Swizz Beatz also won the breakthrough spirit award for his work with the organization. Although being involved in the community doesn't directly generate revenue, it is a free way to spread awareness and also puts you in the customer's good graces.

Here are 10 strategies from Kasseem "Swizz Beatz" Dean that you can use in your own business ventures.

- Reach out to associates to see if they have connections within the industry
- Collaborate with established brands to spread your brand quickly
- Look for ways to build a good image
- Don't limit yourself to a specific niche if you have the opportunity to branch out
- Donate a portion of a specific product to a worthy cause
- Be involved in your community
- Don't let your entire life revolve around the dollar sign

- Keep out of controversy between associates
- Get a mentor
- Observe the blueprints of other brand's success

Marshall "Eminem" Mathers

Net Worth: 115 Million

Even though Eminem's business ventures outside of music are limited, he is still one of the richest rappers in the industry. Eminem got his start under Dr. Dre's label Aftermath Entertainment, and eventually started his own partner label called Shady Records. Eminem also has his own station on Sirius satellite radio called SHADE45. Eminem's one venture outside of music is that he owns a clothing line called Shady Ltd. He also appeared in commercials for Lipton and Chrysler during last year's Superbowl.

Eminem's net worth is probably one of the most impressive on the list given how hard the initial path to break into the industry was for him. He grew up in a mostly African American area of Detroit, which was a mirror image of the rap industry at the time. Therefore, Eminem had to work twice as hard to break into the industry. Eminem's case is a perfect example of how to reach a hard market. One reason he was successful is that he was committed to exposing himself any chance he got, like open mic nights. This is the business equivalent of advertising your product in as many mediums as possible. The more exposure you gain, the better your chances are to succeed.

Eminem is also successful because he is extreme. He thrives off of controversy and uses it to gain exposure. He creates controversy with his lyrics, and this controversy generates buzz. Essentially, Eminem's strategy is to be bold so people have a reason to talk about him. You can use the same strategy to generate buzz about your business. Once in a while make a bold, high risk- high reward move to generate buzz about your brand.

Another smart move by Eminem is that he signed with legendary producer Dr. Dre, thus giving him the credibility he needed in the rap demographic. From there it was easy for Eminem to establish an entirely new sub-industry in rap: the "white rapper" industry. White rappers are now fairly common, especially in the underground rap scene, which is largely due to Eminem's success. Eminem basically established a niche with the white fan base as well as appealed to the rap audience as a whole.

Here are 10 strategies that can help you run your business like Eminem.

- When targeting a hard to reach market, dedication and determination are crucial
- Have complete confidence in your product
- Affiliate with an established brand to gain credibility
- Exploit any niche available
- Be innovative
- Don't be afraid to experiment
- If you can, find a way to market to multiple demographics
- Be unique

- Be bold to generate buzz
- Pay attention to the tastes of your target market

Curtis "50 Cent" Jackson

Net Worth: 100 Million

50 Cent has made a good amount of money in the music industry, and has also done well in his other business ventures. He is the CEO of G Unit clothing, which also sells shoes, accessories, and fragrances. He started the vitamin drink company Vitamin Water, and sold the company for nine figures in 2007. 50 Cent also had a short venture in the headphone business, and is also planning to develop his own nutritional supplement.

50 Cent is a marketing genius, rivaling the entrepreneurial skills of hip-hop moguls like Jay Z and Diddy. First off, he struck marketing gold when he developed Vitamin Water. Vitamin Water is a superb product to market because it offers something for everyone. Those concerned with health are drawn to the product because it contains vitamins. It also tastes well enough to sell to those who just want a refreshing drink. The proverbial Holy Grail of marketing is to create a product everyone wants. Everyone in business should aspire to do what 50 Cent did with Vitamin Water.

Before 50 Cent ventured off into other areas, he had to establish himself as a rapper. 50 Cent put his career on the fast track by affiliating himself with rap legends Eminem and Dr. Dre, which gave him instant credibility. It is always important in business to gain endorsements from companies that will give your product credibility, since customers like to feel like they can trust a company before they make a purchase. 50 Cent's marketing genius is also evident in how he markets his clothing line. He constantly promotes his brand by wearing his own clothes and mentioning his brand in his songs. It also works as a way for fans to feel like they are closer in status to 50 cent when they wear his clothing line. When marketing your product, try to convey it as a status changer. People love to spend money on anything that indicates a high status in society.

50 Cent is also successful because he takes advantage of what's popular. For example, due to shows like the Jersey Shore, many more people are hitting the gym to get fit. 50 Cent realizes this, which is why he wants to develop a nutritional supplement. You can use his strategy by paying attention to current trends and marketing your product accordingly.

A lot can be learned from these 10 strategies 50 Cent uses to be successful.

- Make your product transcend demographics
- Make a product that offers something for everyone
- Make sure your product fits the current market
- Fast track your product by gaining respect from experts
- Build an image that seems authentic to your audience
- Don't be discouraged by a failed business venture
- Use your business intuition
- Market your product as a status enhancer
- Personally endorse your products
- If you sell your business, make sure to get top dollar

Jay "Young Jeezy" Jenkins

Net Worth: 15 Million

In the music business, Young Jeezy is the CEO of his record label Corporate Thug Entertainment. In addition to his record label, he started his own clothing line 8732. He has also inked an advertising deal with Belvedere premium vodka, as well as a venture with Adidas to release his own line of sneakers.

Young Jeezy has always had a head for business, self-proclaiming himself as a corporate thug. One thing that helped Young Jeezy spread his brand so quickly is that he managed to land a group deal with Boyz from da Hood, as well as a solo album. This is the use of collaboration marketing at its finest. Not only does Young Jeezy spread his brand twice as fast, but he also has two separate flows of income. This is a good strategy because if one venture slows down at least you will have another venture generating income. Basically, make sure you don't put all your eggs in one basket. Collaborating is also a good strategy if you need to spread awareness of your brand quickly.

Young Jeezy also has had success because he uses his success in his ventures to fund new projects. He is always looking to expand his brand. Young Jeezy has been around half as long as Rap Moguls like Jay Z and Diddy, but he already has a shoe line, a clothing line, a film career, and an advertising deal. Young Jeezy has been able to accomplish all this by remaining focused and dedicated to constantly expanding his brand. This is a great strategy for any business, since the more markets you have a presence in, the more exposure and profits you'll generate.

Don't be afraid to be innovative in business, as the first business to start a new trend makes the most money. Young Jeezy is also great at cross promoting his ventures. You can purchase your outfit from his clothing line 8732, and his Snowman shoes from Adidas. Essentially Young Jeezy is using two separate ventures to build the bigger picture that is his brand.

Here are 10 strategies that Young Jeezy uses to be successful.

- Take advantage of collaborations
- Be able to succeed individually as well as with a group
- Remain focused on constantly expanding your brand
- The more business ventures you have, the greater your chance of success
- Don't put all of your eggs in one basket
- Do community service to build personal relationships with customers
- Be innovative
- Don't follow trends, start them
- Take advantage of the marketing advantages of social media
- Trust your instincts

Lonnie "Common" Lynn Jr.

Net Worth: 35 Million

Common, formerly known as Common Sense, has been in the Rap industry since the 90's and has had a good amount of success. Common also has a successful film career, starring in movies like Wanted and Smokin' Aces. He has also appeared in advertisements for Gap and designed a line of Italian hats. Common has had success in the writing business as well, as he is the author of a series of children's books. Common is also very active in the community, as he is very involved with PETA and has also started his own charitable foundation in 2007.

Common is different from many Rappers in that he has never sacrificed his style to sell records, yet has still managed to be very successful. Since he got his start as a rapper in the 90's he has been known for lyrics that discuss social issues, even though the popular genre of the time was hardcore Rap. Even though this style of rap was more commercially successful, Common stuck to his guns and kept producing songs with a lyrical message.

Common's strategy paid off when the hardcore style of rap fell out of favor and the market shifted towards desiring songs with a message, which enabled Common to sign his first major record deal. Common used a simple marketing strategy here and that is sticking to his guns. He never gave in by compromising his product to get sales, and it paid off when the market shifted. Although this is a risky strategy, if you really think your strategy is right evaluate the market to see if trends will shift in favor of your product.

Common is also a rarity in the rap world because his image is impeccable. He has never been arrested, and does not use offensive language in his lyrics. In addition, he is very active in the community with PETA. While some people market themselves with controversy, it is much more prudent to take Common's path and avoid controversy. Another strategy Common used for success is that he created a shift in the market with his product. Even if at first glance it seems that the market won't be responsive to your product, you must remain committed to your strategy to shift the market towards your product.

Here are 10 strategies Common uses that can be used for success in any business venture.

- Don't conform to the status quo
- Shift the market towards your product
- Maintain an impeccable image
- Be active in your community
- Be conscious of social issues
- When taking risks, have trust in your intuition
- Learn as much about your market as possible
- Stick to your guns

- Be consistent
- Be philanthropic to build trust in your community

Deandre "Soulja Boy" Way

Net Worth: 23 Million

Soulja Boy burst on the scene at the tender age of 18 when he released his first single "Crank That". Soulja Boy also has his own record label, called Stacks on Deck Entertainment. Outside of the music industry, Soulja Boy has partnered with apparel company Yums to create his own line of clothing and shoes. Soulja Boy also has endorsement deals with Cricket Mobile, and his own iPhone app called Romplr.

Soulja Boy is an interesting figure in the rap industry. One side of the industry says Soulja Boy sucked the substance out of hip hop and reduced it to a gimmick; while others think Soulja Boy is a marketing genius for providing a product that appealed to a wide audience. What Soulja Boy did may have caused others in the industry to hate him, but it made him rich. This is a good strategy to use in business, but remember to make sure that the reward of the potential profit is worth the backlash you'll receive.

Another reason why Soulja Boy is a huge success is that he is a master of social media marketing. He originally released what would become a platinum selling song as a free YouTube video. Rather than waiting for the tedious process of traditional marketing, Soulja Boy got his product out instantly and free of charge. In today's digital age, every business should have a social media presence. It provides you instant feedback from customers, as well as a place for all of your customers to get instant updates about your brand.

Soulja Boy is also successful because his product is designed specifically to appeal to as many people as possible. He has admitted that his songs are not the most lyrical ones out there, but that is by design. The lesson to be learned here is that you must take into account how complex or sophisticated your product is when figuring out your target market.

Soulja boy is also successful because he uses the internet to market himself. For example, he used the website Saynow.com to promote his last album, which gives artists their own phone number that they call and leave a voicemail that will then be sent to all of their followers.

Here are 10 strategies that you can take from Soulja Boy to help successfully run your business.

- Be innovative
- Gain exposure
- Take advantage of the internet
- It doesn't matter what others think if you feel you will be successful
- Master social media
- Try new social media methods

- Provide your audience with product they want
- Trust your intuition
- Try to go viral with web content
- Stay focused and brush off critics

Faheem "T Pain" Najm

Net Worth: 30 Million

T Pain is a relative newcomer compared to other Rappers on this list, but he is quickly making a name for himself. He is responsible for popularizing the auto tune pitch effect heard in most songs today, and consequently enjoyed a lucrative partnership with the company that produces the auto tune software, Antares. T Pain also has recently released an iPhone app called " I Am T Pain", which allows you to add auto tune to your voice.

Without a doubt, the key factor to T Pain's success is his ability to squeeze every last dollar of value out of a product. T Pain was the first rapper to use auto tune on a song and every song he has recorded uses auto tune. His first song was a monster hit and the use of auto tune subsequently spread throughout the industry. T Pain predicted this would happen, so he established a partnership with the developer of the auto tune software, Antares. Recently, he further capitalized on the auto tune phenomenon by creating an iPhone app called " I Am T Pain", allowing users to add auto tune to their voice. The strategy T Pain is using here is increasing the market life of his product. You can use this strategy to sustain the popularity of your products by creating innovative ways for your customer to interact with your product.

T Pain is also smart because he takes advantage of Application marketing, which is the next big industry given the current popularity of Smartphones. Figure out a way to develop an app that your customers can download to their phones. After all, a person's phone is usually the one piece of technology they have with them at all times.

T Pain is also so good at reading his target market that he knew what they wanted before they did. In other words, he created something that no one heard before and everyone ended up loving. He has gained massive brand exposure because people saw how successful auto tune sold, so they wanted him on their songs. Your goal should be to be able to establish your product and brand as one that companies want to affiliate with, since you can provide them with good exposure.

Here are 10 tips you can take from T Pain and use in your own business.

- Set a new standard with your product
- Sustain your brand popularity by creating new ways to interact with your product
- Embrace criticism
- Create a brand that people want to affiliate with
- Take advantage of your popularity
- Develop a Smartphone application
- Know what your customers want
- Develop something original
- Maximize affiliation opportunities
- You can never have too much exposure

Jonathan "Lil Jon" Smith

Net Worth: 25 Million

Lil Jon has been in the music industry since 1997 and is one of the first Southern Rappers to gain mainstream popularity. He has had solo success as well as group success with Lil Jon and the Eastside Boyz. His other business ventures include Crunk energy drink, as well as a line of Oakley sunglasses. He also started a wine label in 2008 called Little Jonathan. In addition to the business world, Lil Jon has also appeared on Celebrity Apprentice, making it to the final four before being eliminated.

Lil Jon is another rapper who managed to give his audience what they wanted before they knew they wanted it. Although he does have a rap group, Lil Jon and the Eastside Boyz, Lil Jon basically gained his popularity from uttering two words: "yeah" and "okay." Lil Jon is a great testament that delivery can make or break you when marketing a product. Not many people would be able to take these two words and make themselves millions, as it is how Lil Jon delivers them that makes him so popular. This is a good strategy to use in your business as it promotes creative problem solving. It forces you to evaluate your product to develop the best marketing plan possible.

Lil Jon is also successful because he capitalized on his peak popularity by affiliating with countless artists. Every artist wanted Lil Jon to go "yeah" on their track because they knew that that's what the customer wanted. A great business strategy is to always strive to make your brand one that is appealing for affiliation.

Lil Jon is also great at cross promotion, which is evident in his Crunk energy drink venture. Lil Jon popularized the term crunk, which means energy, into mainstream slang. Lil Jon took advantage of the term's popularity and named his energy drink Crunk. This is genius on his part because he has a built-in marketing plan just by choosing the right name for his product. People who have started using the word crunk will purchase Crunk whenever they want an energy drink. If your business already has a successful product, use that product to market your new product.

Finally, Lil Jon is successful because he takes risks in unconventional markets, which is what he did with his brand of wine, Little Jonathan. Many rappers have cognacs and malt liquors, but Lil Jon is the first rapper to branch into the wine industry. Being a trendsetter is a great business strategy as those who start trends make the most money.

Here are 10 ways you can run your business like Lil Jon.

- Deliver your product in the best way possible
- Know what your audience wants

- Diversify your business
- Take advantage of up and coming trends
- Be innovative
- Take risks
- Don't be afraid to enter unconventional markets
- Trust your instincts
- Be a trendsetter
- Think long term

Conclusion

From Jay Z all the way down to Lil Jon, these men have proven that they are not just entertainers, but businessmen dedicated to making the most money as possible off of their brand. While many of their roads to success cross paths, each rapper on this list provides unique techniques for success that can be adapted for use in the business world.

References

Greenburg, Z. (2010). The crunk life: rapper lil jon on how he's creating a diversified portfolio. DailyFinance, Retrieved from http://www.dailyfinance.com/2010/05/14/the-crunk-life-rapper-lil-jon-on-how-hes-creating-a-diversifie/

Hazelwood, J. (2010, November 3rd). What you could learn from Soulja Boy's social media marketing success. http://www.blackenterprise.com/2010/11/03/what-you-could-learn-from-soulja-boys-social-media-marketing-success/,

Ramirez, E. (2011, May 24th). Chris lightly talks 50 cent's next business possibilites's [Web log message]. Retrieved from http://www.billboard.biz/bbbiz/genre/randb-hip-hop/chris-lighty-on-50-cent-s-next-business-1005199402.story

Johnson, L. (2006, November 15th). Much ado about jay z [Web log message]. Retrieved from http://www.fastcompany.com/blog/lynne-d-johnson/digital-media-diva/much-ado-about-jay-z

http://www.evancarmichael.com/Famous-Entrepreneurs/622/Its-a-Rap-How-Sean-Combs-Achieved-Success.html

All Net Worth's are from: www.therichest.org

All biographical information and information on business ventures from: www.wikipedia.org

About Minute Help Press

Minute Help Press is building a library of books for people with only minutes to spare. Follow @minutehelp on Twitter to receive the latest information about free and paid publications from Minute Help Press, or visit minutehelpguides.com.

Made in the USA
Middletown, DE
27 November 2015